Fires

Book 3
The Hare, and Other Tales

by

Wilfrid Wilson Gibson

Fires
Book 3
The Hare, and Other Tales
by Wilfrid Wilson Gibson

Copyright © 2024

All Rights reserved.

ISBN: 978-93-61424-40-3

Published by

DOUBLE 9 BOOKS

2/13-B, Ansari Road
Daryaganj, New Delhi – 110002
info@double9books.com
www.double9books.com
Tel. 011-40042856

ABOUT THE AUTHOR

Wilfrid Wilson Gibson, a notable English poet of the early 20th century, left an indelible mark on literature with his profound insights into the human condition. Born in 1878, Gibson's works often explored themes of nature, social injustice, and the struggles of the working class. Among his notable works, "Fires: The Stone, and Other Tales" stands out as a masterpiece of poetry and prose. In "Fires," Gibson presents a collection of poignant tales that delve into the complexities of life, each story serving as a metaphorical flame illuminating the human experience. The subtitle, "The Stone, and Other Tales," hints at the varied subjects explored within the book, from the enduring resilience of the human spirit to the harsh realities of existence. Gibson's mastery lies in his ability to weave together lyrical language with profound insights, creating a tapestry of emotion and imagery that resonates deeply with readers. Through his stories, he invites readers to confront universal truths and contemplate the intricacies of the human condition. "Fires: The Stone, and Other Tales" stands as a testament to Gibson's literary talent and his ability to capture the essence of life in all its beauty and complexity. With its evocative prose and timeless themes, this masterpiece continues to inspire and move readers around the world.

CONTENTS

THE DANCING SEAL

When we were building Skua Light--
The first men who had lived a night
Upon that deep-sea Isle--
As soon as chisel touched the stone,
The friendly seals would come ashore;
And sit and watch us all the while,
As though they'd not seen men before;
And so, poor beasts, had never known
Men had the heart to do them harm.
They'd little cause to feel alarm
With us, for we were glad to find
Some friendliness in that strange sea;
Only too pleased to let them be
And sit as long as they'd a mind
To watch us: for their eyes were kind
Like women's eyes, it seemed to me.

So, hour on hour, they sat: I think
They liked to hear the chisels' clink:
And when the boy sang loud and clear,
They scrambled closer in to hear;
And if he whistled sweet and shrill,
The queer beasts shuffled nearer still:
But every sleek and sheeny skin
Was mad to hear his violin.

When, work all over for the day,
He'd take his fiddle down and play
His merry tunes beside the sea,

Their eyes grew brighter and more bright,
And burned and twinkled merrily:
And as I watched them one still night,
And saw their eager sparkling eyes,
I felt those lively seals would rise
Some shiny night ere he could know,
And dance about him, heel and toe,
Unto the fiddle's heady tune.

And at the rising of the moon,
Half-daft, I took my stand before
A young seal lying on the shore;
And called on her to dance with me.
And it seemed hardly strange when she
Stood up before me suddenly,
And shed her black and sheeny skin;
And smiled, all eager to begin...
And I was dancing, heel and toe,
With a young maiden white as snow,
Unto a crazy violin.

We danced beneath the dancing moon,
All night, beside the dancing sea,
With tripping toes and skipping heels:
And all about us friendly seals
Like Christian folk were dancing reels
Unto the fiddle's endless tune
That kept on spinning merrily
As though it never meant to stop.
And never once the snow-white maid
A moment stayed
To take a breath,
Though I was fit to drop:
And while those wild eyes challenged me,
I knew as well as well could be
I must keep step with that young girl,
Though we should dance to death.

Then with a skirl
The fiddle broke:
The moon went out:
The sea stopped dead:
And, in a twinkling, all the rout
Of dancing folk had fled...
And in the chill bleak dawn I woke
Upon the naked rock, alone.

They've brought me far from Skua Isle...
I laugh to think they do not know
That as, all day, I chip the stone,
Among my fellows here inland,
I smell the sea-wrack on the shore...
And see her snowy-tossing hand,
And meet again her merry smile...
And dream I'm dancing all the while,
I'm dancing ever, heel and toe,
With a seal-maiden, white as snow,
On that moonshiny Island-strand,
For ever and for evermore.

THE SLAG

Among bleak hills of mounded slag they walked,
'Neath sullen evening skies that seemed to sag
O'er-burdened by the belching smoke, and lie
Upon their aching foreheads, dense and dank,
Till both felt youth within them fail and flag--
Even as the flame which shot a fiery rag
A fluttering moment through the murky sky
Above the black blast-furnaces, then sank
Again beneath the iron bell close-bound--
And it was all that they could do to drag
Themselves along, 'neath that dead-weight of smoke,
Over the cinder-blasted, barren ground.
Though fitfully and fretfully she talked,
He never turned his eyes to her, or spoke:
And as he slouched with her along the track
That skirted a stupendous, lowering mound,
With listless eyes, and o'er-strained sinews slack,
She bit a petted, puckered lip, and frowned
To think she ever should be walking out
With this tongue-tied, slow-witted, hulking lout,
As cold and dull and lifeless as the slag.

And, all on edge, o'erwrought by the crampt day
Of crouched, close stitching at her dull machine,
It seemed to her a girl of seventeen
Should have, at least, an hour of careless talking--
Should have, at least, an hour of life, out walking
Beside a lover, mettlesome and gay--
Not through her too short freedom doomed to lag

Beside a sparkless giant, glum and grim,
Till all her eager youth should waste away.
Yet, even as she looked askance at him--
Well-knit, big-thewed, broad-chested, steady-eyed--
She dimly knew of depths she could not sound
In this strong lover, silent at her side:
And, once again, her heart was touched with pride
To think that he was hers, this strapping lad--
Black-haired, close-cropt, clean-skinned, and neatly clad...
His crimson neckerchief, so smartly tied--
And hers alone, and more than all she had
In all the world to her ... and yet, so grave!
If he would only shew that he was glad
To be with her--a gleam, a spark of fire,
A spurt of flame to shoot into the night,
A moment through the murky heavens to wave
An eager beacon of enkindling light
In answer to her young heart's quick desire!

Yet, though he walked with dreaming eyes agaze,
As, deep within a mound of slag, a core
Of unseen fire may smoulder many days,
Till suddenly the whole heap glow ablaze,
That seemed, but now, dead cinder, grey and cold,
Life smouldered in his heart. The fire he fed
Day-long in the tall furnace just ahead
From that frail gallery slung against the sky
Had burned through all his being, till the ore
Glowed in him. Though no surface-stream of gold
Quick-molten slag of speech was his to spill
Unceasingly, the burning metal still
Seethed in him, from the broken furnace-side
To burst at any moment in a tide
Of white-hot molten iron o'er the mould...

But still he spoke no word as they strolled on
Into the early-gathering Winter night:
And, as she watched the leaping furnace-light,
She had no thought of smouldering fires unseen...
The daylong clattering whirr of her machine
Hummed in her ears again--the straining thread
And stabbing needle starting through her head--
Until the last dull gleam of day was gone...

When, all at once, upon the right,
A crackling crash, a blinding flare...
A shower of cinders through the air...
A grind of blocks of slag aslide...
And, far above them, in the night,
The looming heap had opened wide
About a fiery, gaping pit...
And, startled and aghast at it,
With clasping hands they stood astare,
And gazed upon the awful glare:
And, as she felt him clutch her hand,
She seemed to know her heart's desire,
For evermore with him to stand
In that enkindling blaze of fire...
When, suddenly, he left her side;
And started scrambling up the heap:
And, looking up, with stifled cry,
She saw, against the glowing sky,
Almost upon the pit's red brink,
A little lad, stock-still with fright
Before the blazing pit of dread
Agape before him in the night,
Where, playing castles on the height
Since noon, he'd fallen, spent, asleep
And dreaming he was home in bed...

With brain afire, too strained to think,
She watched her lover climb and leap
From jag to jag
Of broken slag...
And still he only seemed to creep...
She felt that he would never reach
That little lad, though he should climb
Until the very end of time...
And, as she looked, the burning breach
Gaped suddenly more wide...
The slag again began to slide,
And crash into the pit,
Until the dazed lad's feet
Stood on the edge of it.
She saw him reel and fall...
And thought him done for ... then
Her lover, brave and tall,
Against the glare and heat,
A very fire-bright god of men!
He stooped ... and now she knew the lad
Was safe with Robert, after all.

And while she watched, a throng of folk
Attracted by the crash and flare,
Had gathered round, though no one spoke
But all stood terror-stricken there,
With lifted eyes and indrawn breath,
Until the lad was snatched from death
Upon the very pit's edge, when,
As Robert picked him up, and turned,
A sigh ran through the crowd; and fear
Gave place to joy, as cheer on cheer
Sang through the kindled air...

But still she never uttered word,
As though she neither saw nor heard;

Till as, at last, her lad drew near,
She saw him bend with tender care
Over the sobbing child who lay
Safe in his arms, and hug him tight
Against his breast--his brow alight
With eager, loving eyes that burned
In his transfigured face aflame...
And even when the parents came
It almost seemed that he was loth
To yield them up their little son;
As though the lad were his by right
Of rescue, from the pit's edge won.
Then, as his eyes met hers, she felt
An answering thrill of tenderness
Run, quickening, through her breast; and both
Stood quivering there, with envious eyes,
And stricken with a strange distress,
As quickly homeward through the night
The happy parents bore their boy...

And then, about her reeling bright,
The whole night seemed to her to melt
In one fierce, fiery flood of joy.

DEVIL'S EDGE

All night I lay on Devil's Edge,
Along an overhanging ledge
Between the sky and sea:
And as I rested 'waiting sleep,
The windless sky and soundless deep
In one dim, blue infinity
Of starry peace encompassed me.

And I remembered, drowsily,
How 'mid the hills last night I 'd lain
Beside a singing moorland burn;
And waked at dawn, to feel the rain
Fall on my face, as on the fern
That drooped about my heather-bed:
And how by noon the wind had blown
The last grey shred from out the sky,
And blew my homespun jacket dry,
As I stood on the topmost stone
That crowns the cairn on Hawkshaw Head,
And caught a gleam of far-off sea;
And heard the wind sing in the bent
Like those far waters calling me:
When, my heart answering to the call,
I followed down the seaward stream,
By silent pool and singing fall;
Till with a quiet, keen content,
I watched the sun, a crimson ball,
Shoot through grey seas a fiery gleam,
Then sink in opal deeps from sight.

And with the coming on of night,
The wind had dropped: and as I lay,
Retracing all the happy day,
And gazing long and dreamily
Across the dim, unsounding sea,
Over the far horizon came
A sudden sail of amber flame;
And soon the new moon rode on high
Through cloudless deeps of crystal sky.

Too holy seemed the night for sleep:
And yet, I must have slept, it seems;
For, suddenly, I woke to hear
A strange voice singing, shrill and clear,
Down in a gully black and deep
That cleft the beetling crag in twain.
It seemed the very voice of dreams
That drive hag-ridden souls in fear
Through echoing, unearthly vales,
To plunge in black, slow-crawling streams,
Seeking to drown that cry, in vain...
Or some sea creature's voice that wails
Through blind, white banks of fog unlifting
To God-forgotten sailors drifting
Rudderless to death...
And as I heard,
Though no wind stirred,
An icy breath
Was in my hair...
And clutched my heart with cold despair...
But, as the wild song died away,
There came a faltering break
That shivered to a sobbing fall;
And seemed half-human, after all...

And yet, what foot could find a track
In that deep gully, sheer and black...
And singing wildly in the night!
So, wondering I lay awake,
Until the coming of the light
Brought day's familiar presence back.

Down by the harbour-mouth that day,
A fisher told the tale to me.
Three months before, while out at sea,
Young Philip Burn was lost, though how,
None knew, and none would ever know.
The boat becalmed at noonday lay...
And not a ripple on the sea...
And Philip standing in the bow,
When his six comrades went below
To sleep away an hour or so,
Dog-tired with working day and night,
While he kept watch ... and not a sound
They heard, until, at set of sun
They woke; and coming up, they found
The deck was empty, Philip gone...
Yet not another boat in sight...
And not a ripple on the sea.
How he had vanished, none could tell.
They only knew the lad was dead
They'd left but now, alive and well...
And he, poor fellow, newly-wed...
And when they broke the news to her,
She spoke no word to anyone:
But sat all day, and would not stir--
Just staring, staring in the fire,
With eyes that never seemed to tire;
Until, at last, the day was done,
And darkness came; when she would rise,

And seek the door with queer, wild eyes;
And wander singing all the night
Unearthly songs beside the sea:
But always the first blink of light
Would find her back at her own door.

'Twas Winter when I came once more
To that old village by the shore:
And as, at night, I climbed the street,
I heard a singing, low and sweet,
Within a cottage near at hand:
And I was glad awhile to stand
And listen by the glowing pane:
And as I hearkened, that sweet strain
Brought back the night when I had lain
Awake on Devil's Edge...
And now I knew the voice again,
So different, free of pain and fear--
Its terror turned to tenderness--
And yet the same voice none the less,
Though singing now so true and clear
And drawing nigh the window-ledge,
I watched the mother sing to rest
The baby snuggling to her breast.

THE LILAC TREE

"I planted her the lilac tree
Upon our wedding day:
But, when the time of blossom came,
With her dead babe she lay...
And, as I stood beside the bed,
The scent of lilac filled the room:
And always when I smell the bloom,
I think upon the dead."

He spoke: and, speaking, sauntered on,
The young girl by his side:
And then they talked no more of death,
But only of the happy things
That burst their buds, and spread their wings,
And break in song at Whitsuntide,
That burst to bloom at Whitsuntide,
And bring the summer in a breath.

And, as they talked, the young girl's life
Broke into bloom and song;
And, one with all the happy things
That burst their buds, and spread their wings,
Her very blood was singing,
And at her pulses ringing;
Life tingled through her, sweet and strong,
From secret sources springing:
And, all at once, a quickening strife
Of hopes and fears was in her heart,
Where only wondering joy had been;

And, kindling with a sudden light,
Her eyes had sight
Of things unseen:
And, in a flash, a woman grown,
With pangs of knowledge, fierce and keen,
She knew strange things unknown.

A year went by: at Whitsuntide,
He brought her home, a bride.

He planted her no lilac tree
Upon their wedding day:
And strange distress came over her,
As on the bed she lay:
For as he stood beside the bed,
The scent of lilac filled the room.
Her heart knew well he smelt the bloom,
And thought upon the dead.
Yet, she was glad to be his wife:
And when the blossom-time was past,
Her days no more were overcast;
And deep she drank of life:
And, thronged with happy household cares,
Her busy days went pleasantly:
Her foot was light upon the stairs;
And every room rang merrily,
And merrily, and merrily,
With song and mirth, for unto her
His heart seemed hers, and hers alone:
Until new dreams began to stir
Her wondering breast with bliss unknown
Of some new miracle to be:
And, though she moved more quietly,
And seldom sang, yet, happily,
From happy dawn to happy night
The mother's eyes shone bright.

And so I dropped on hands and knees,
And crawled along the gallery,
Beneath the smoke, that I might see
What ailed: and as I crept, half-blind,
With smarting eyes, and breath awheeze,
I scarcely knew what I should find.
At times, I thought I'd never know...
And 'twas already quite an age
Since I set out ... I felt as though
I had been crawling all my life
Beneath the stifling cloud of smoke
That clung about me fit to choke:
And when, at last, I'd struggled here,
'Twas long ere I could see things clear...
That he was lying here ... and he
Was dead ... and burning like a tree...
A tree-trunk soaked in oil ... No doubt,
The engine had caught fire, somehow;
And when he tried to put it out,
His greasy clothes had caught ... and now
As fine a lad as you could see...
And such a lad for singing ... I
Had heard him when I worked hard by;
And often quiet I would sit
To hear him, singing in the pit,
As though his heart knew naught of it,
And life was nothing but a song.

"He'd not been working with us long:
And little of his ways I knew:
But, when I'd got him up, at last;
And he was lying in the shed,
The sweet song silent in his breast;
And there was nothing more to do:
The notion came into my head

That he had always been well-dressed;
And seemed a neat and thrifty lad...
And lived in lodgings ... so, maybe,
Would carry on him all he had.
So, back into the cage I stepped:
And, when it reached the bottom, crept
Along the gallery again
And, in the dust where he had lain,
I rummaged, until I found all
That from his burning pockets fell.
And when it seemed there was no more,
I thought how, happy and alive,
And recking naught what might befall,
He, too, for all that I could tell,
Just where I stood, had reckoned o'er
That four-pound-seventeen-and-five.

"Aye, like enough ... for soon we heard
That in a week he'd looked to wed.
He'd meant to give the girl that night
The money to buy furniture.
She came, and watched till morning-light
Beside the body in the shed:
Then rose: and took, without a word,
The money he had left for her."

Then, as I wandered through the rain,
I seemed to stand in awe again
Beside that lonely garret-bed.
And it was good to think the dead
Had known the wealth she would not spend
To keep a little while alive--
His four-pound-seventeen-and-five--
Would buy her houseroom in the end.

THE SNOW

Just as the school came out,
The first white flakes were drifting round about:
And all the children shouted with delight
To see such flakes, so big, so white,
Tumbling from a cloud so black,
And whirling helter-skelter
Across the windy moor:
And as they saw the light flakes race,
Started off in headlong chase,
Swooping on them with a shout,
When they seemed to drop for shelter
Underneath the dry-stone wall.

And then the master, at the schoolhouse door,
Called out to them to hurry home, before
The storm should come on worse: and watched till all
Had started off by road or moorland track:
When, turning to his wife, he said:
It looked like dirty weather overhead:
He thought 'twould be a heavy fall,
And threatened for a roughish night;
But they would all reach home in broad daylight.
'Twas early, yet; he'd let the school out soon;
As it had looked so lowering since forenoon;
And many had a goodish step to go:
And it was but ill-travelling in the snow.
Then by the fire he settled down to read;
And to the weather paid no further heed.

And, on their road home, full three miles away,
John, and his little sister, Janey, started;
And, at the setting out, were happy-hearted
To be let loose into a world so gay,
With jolly winds and frisking flakes at play
That flicked your cheek, and whistled in your teeth:
And now hard on each other's heels they darted
To catch a flake that floated like a feather,
Then dropt to nestle in a clump of heather;
And often tumbled both together
Into a deep delicious bed
Of brown and springy heath.
But, when the sky grew blacker overhead,
As if it were the coming on of night,
And every little hill, well-known to sight,
Looked big and strange in its new fleece of white;
And as yet faster and more thickly
The big flakes fell,
To John the thought came that it might be well
To hurry home; so, striding on before,
He set a steady face across the moor;
And called to Janey she must come more quickly.

The wind soon dropped: and fine and dry the snow
Came whispering down about them, as they trudged
And, when they'd travelled for a mile or so,
They found it ankle-deep: for here the storm
Had started long before it reached the school:
And, as he felt the dry flakes tingling warm
Upon his cheek, and set him all aglow,
John in his manly pride, a little grudged
That now and then he had to wait awhile
For Janey, lagging like a little fool:
But, when they'd covered near another mile
Through that bewildering white without a sound,

Save rustling, rustling, rustling all around;
And all his well-known world, so queer and dim,
He waited until she caught up to him;
And felt quite glad that he was not alone.

And when they reached the low, half-buried stone
That marked where some old shepherd had been found,
Lost in the snow in seeking his lost sheep,
One wild March night, full forty years ago,
He wished, and wished, that they were safe and sound
In their own house: and as the snow got deeper,
And every little bank seemed strangely steeper,
He thought, and thought of that lost sleeper;
And saw him lying in the snow,
Till every fleecy clump of heath
Seemed to shroud a man beneath;
And now his blood went hot and cold
Through very fear of that dread sight;
And then he felt that, in sheer fright,
He must take to his heels in flight,
He cared not whither, so that it might be
Where there were no more bundles, cold and white,
Like sheeted bodies, plain to see.
And, all on edge, he turned to chide
His sister, dragging at his side:
But, when he found that she was crying,
Because her feet and hands were cold,
He quite forgot to scold:
And spoke kind words of cheer to her:
And saw no more dead shepherds lying
In any snowy clump of heather.
So, hand in hand, they trudged together,
Through that strange world of drifting gloam,
Sharp-set and longing sore for home.

And John remembered how that morning,
When they set out the sky was blue--
Clean, cloudless blue; and gave no warning;
And how through air as clear as glass,
The far-off hills he knew
Looked strangely near; and glittered brightly;
Each sprig of heath and blade of grass
In the cold wind blowing lightly,
Each clump of green and crimson moss
Sparkling in the wintry sun.

But now, as they toiled home, across
These unfamiliar fells, nigh done,
The wind again began to blow;
And thicker, thicker fell the snow:
Till Janey sank, too numb to stir:
When John stooped down, and lifted her,
To carry her upon his back.
And then his head began to tire:
And soon he seemed to lose the track...
And now the world was all afire...
Now dazzling white, now dazzling black...
And then, through some strange land of light,
Where clouds of butterflies all white,
Fluttered and flickered all about,
Dancing ever in and out,
He wandered, blinded by white wings,
That rustled, rustled in his ears
With cold, uncanny whisperings...
And then it seemed his bones must crack
With that dead weight upon his back...
When, on his cheek, he felt warm tears,
And a cold tangle of wet hair;
And knew 'twas Janey weeping there:
And, taking heart, he stumbled on,

While in his breast the hearthlight shone:
And it was all of his desire
To sit once more before the fire;
And feel the friendly glowing heat.
But, as he strove with fumbling feet,
It seemed that he would never find
Again that cheery hearth and kind;
But wander ever, bent and blind,
Beneath his burden through the night
Of dreadful, spangly, whispering white.
The wind rose; and the dry snow drifted
In little eddies round the track:
And when, at last, the dark cloud rifted,
He saw a strange lough, lying cold and black,
'Mid unknown, ghostly hills; and knew
That they were lost: and once again,
The snow closed in: and swept from view
The dead black water and strange fells.

But still he struggled on: and then,
When he seemed climbing up an endless steep
And ever slipping, sliding back,
With ankles aching like to crack,
And only longed for sleep;
He heard a tinkling sound of bells,
That kept on ringing, ringing, ringing,
Until his dizzy head was singing;
And he could think of nothing else:
And then it seemed the weight was lifted
From off his back; and on the ground
His sister stood, while, all around
Were giants clad in coats of wool,
With big, curled horns, and queer black faces,
Who bobbed and curtsied in their places,
With blazing eyes and strange grimaces;

But never made a sound;
Then nearly shook themselves to pieces,
Shedding round a smell of warm, wet fleeces:
Then one it seemed as if he knew,
Looking like the old lame ewe,
Began to bite his coat, and pull
Till he could hardly stand: its eyes
Glowing to a monstrous size,
Till they were like a lantern light
Burning brightly through the night...
When someone stooped from out the sky,
To rescue him; and set him high:
And he was riding, snug and warm,
In some king's chariot through the storm,
Without a sound of wheel or hoof--
In some king's chariot, filled with straw,
And he would nevermore be cold...

And then with wondering eyes he saw
Deep caverns of pure burning gold;
And knew himself in fairyland:
But when he stretched an eager hand
To touch the glowing walls, he felt
A queer warm puff, as though of fire...
And suddenly he smelt
The reek of peat; and looking higher,
He saw the old, black porridge-kettle,
Hanging from the cavern roof,
Hanging on its own black crook:
And he was lying on the settle,
While by his side,
With tender look,
His mother knelt;
And he had only one desire
In all the world; and 'twas to fling

His arms about her neck, and hide
His happy tears upon her breast.
And as to her he closely pressed,
He heard his merry father sing:
"There was a silly sleepyhead,
Who thought he'd like to go to bed:
So in a stell he went to sleep,
And snored among the other sheep."

And then his mother gently said:
"Nay, father: do not tease him now:
He's quite worn out: and needs a deal
Of quiet sleep: and, after all,
He brought his sister safe from school."
And now he felt her warm tears fall
Upon his cheek: and thrilled to feel
His father's hand on his hot brow,
And hear him say: "The lad's no fool."

RED FOX

I hated him ... his beard was red...
Red fox, red thief! ... Ah, God, that she--
She with the proud and lifted head
That never stooped to glance at me--
So fair and fancy-free, should wed
A slinking dog-fox such as he!

Was it last night I hated him?
Last night? It seems an age ago...
At whiles, my mind comes over dim
As if God's breath ... yet, ever slow
And dull, too dull she ... limb from limb
Last night I could have torn him, so!

My lonely bed was fire and ice.
I could not sleep. I could not lie.
I shut my hot eyes once or twice...
And saw a red fox slinking by...
A red dog-fox that turned back thrice
To mock me with a merry eye.

And so I rose to pace the floor...
And, ere I knew, my clothes were on...
And as I stood outside the door,
Cold in the Summer moonlight shone
The gleaming barrel ... and no more
I feared the fox, for fear was one.

"The best of friends," I said, "must part..."

"The best of friends must part," I said:
And like the creaking of a cart
The words went wheeling through my head.
"The best of friends..." and, in my heart,
Red fox, already lying dead!

I took the trackway through the wood.
Red fox had sought a woodland den,
When she ... when she ... but, 'twas not good
To think too much on her just then...
The woman must beware, who stood
Between two stark and fearless men.

The pathway took a sudden turn...
And in a trice my steps were stayed.
Before me, in the moonlit fern,
A young dog-fox and vixen played
With their red cubs beside the burn...
And I stood trembling and afraid.

They frolicked in the warm moonlight--
A scuffling heap of heads and heels...
A rascal rush ... a playful bite...
A scuttling brush, and frightened squeals...
A flash of teeth ... a show of fight...
Then lively as a bunch of eels

Once more they gambolled in the brake,
And tumbled headlong in the stream,
Then scrambled gasping out to shake
Their sleek, wet, furry coats agleam.
I watched them, fearful and awake...
I watched them, hateless and adream.

The dog-fox gave a bark, and then
All ran to him: and, full of pride,
He took the trackway up the glen,

His family trotting by his side:
The young cubs nosing for the den,
With trailing brushes, sleepy-eyed.

And then it seems I must have slept--
Dropt dead asleep ... dropt dead outworn.
I wakened, as the first gleam crept
Among the fern, and it was morn...
God's eye about their home had kept
Good watch, the night her son was born.

THE OVENS

He trailed along the cinder-track
Beside the sleek canal, whose black
Cold, slinking waters shivered back
Each frosty spark of starry light;
And each star pricked, an icy pin,
Through his old jacket worn and thin:
The raw wind rasped his shrinking skin
As if stark naked to its bite;
Yet, cutting through him like a knife,
It would not cut the thread of life;
But only turned his feet to stones
With red-hot soles, that weighed like lead
In his old broken boots. His head,
Sunk low upon his sunken chest,
Was but a burning, icy ache
That strained a skull which would not break
To let him tumble down to rest.
He felt the cold stars in his bones:
And only wished that he were dead,
With no curst searching wind to shred
The very flesh from off his bones--
No wind to whistle through his bones,
His naked, icy, burning bones:
When, looking up, he saw, ahead,
The far coke-ovens' glowing light
That burnt a red hole in the night.
And but to snooze beside that fire

Was all the heaven of his desire...
To tread no more this cursed track
Of crunching cinders, through a black
And blasted world of cinder-heaps,
Beside a sleek canal that creeps
Like crawling ice through every bone,
Beneath the cruel stars, alone
With this hell-raking wind that sets
The cold teeth rattling castanets...
Yea, heaven, indeed, that core of red
In night's black heart that seemed quite dead.
Though still far off, the crimson glow
Through his chilled veins began to flow,
And fill his shrivelled heart with heat;
And, as he dragged his senseless feet,
That lagged as though to hold him back
In cold, eternal hell of black,
With heaven before him, blazing red,
The set eyes staring in his head
Were held by spell of fire quite blind
To that black world that fell behind,
A cindery wilderness of death;
As he drew slowly near and nearer,
And saw the ovens glowing clearer--
Low-domed and humming hives of heat--
And felt the blast of burning breath
That quivered from each white-hot brick:
Till, blinded by the blaze, and sick
He dropped into a welcome seat
Of warm white ashes, sinking low
To soak his body in the glow
That shot him through with prickling pain,
An eager agony of fire,
Delicious after the cold ache,

And scorched his tingling, frosted skin.
Then gradually the anguish passed;
And blissfully he lay, at last,
Without an unfulfilled desire,
His grateful body drinking in
Warm, blessed, snug forgetfulness.
And yet, with staring eyes awake,
As though no drench of heat could slake
His thirst for fire, he watched a red
Hot eye that burned within a chink
Between the bricks: while overhead
The quivering stream of hot, gold air
Surged up to quench the cold starlight.
His brain, too numbed and dull to think
Throughout the day, in that fierce glare
Awoke, at last, with startled stare
Of pitiless, insistent sight
That stript the stark, mean, bitter strife
Of his poor, broken, wasted life,
Crippled from birth, and struggling on,
The last, least shred of hope long gone,
To some unknown, black, bitter end.
But, even as he looked, his brain
Sank back to sightless sloth again;
Then, all at once, he seemed to choke;
And knew it was the stealthy stife
And deadly fume of burning coke
That filled his lungs, and seemed to soak
Through every pore, until the blood
Grew thick and heavy in his veins,
And he could scarcely draw a breath.
He lay, and murmured drowsily,
With closing eyes: "If this be death,
It's snug and easy ... let it come...

For life is cold and hard ... the flood
Is rising with the heavy rains
That pour and pour ... that damned old drum,
Why ever can't they let it be...
Beat-beating, beating, beating, beat..."
Then, suddenly, he sat upright,
For, close behind him in the night,
He heard a breathing loud and deep,
And caught a whiff of burning leather.
He shook himself alive, and turned;
And on a heap of ashes white,
O'ercome by the full blast of heat,
Where fieriest the dread blaze burned,
He saw a young girl stretched in sleep.
He sat awhile with heavy gaze
Fixed on her in a dull amaze,
Until he saw her scorched boots smoking:
Then, whispering huskily: "She's dying,
While I look on and watch her choking!"
He roused: and pulled himself together:
And rose, and went where she was lying:
And, bending o'er the senseless lass,
In his weak arms he lifted her;
And bore her out beyond the glare,
Beyond the stealthy, stifling gas,
Into the fresh and eager air:
And laid her gently on the ground
Beneath the cold and starry sky:
And did his best to bring her round;
Though still, for all that he could try,
She seemed, with each deep-labouring breath
Just brought up on the brink of death.
He sought, and found an icy pool,
Though he had but a cap to fill,

And bathed her hands and face, until
The troubled breath was quieter,
And her flushed forehead felt quite cool:
And then he saw an eyelid stir;
And shivering she sat up at last,
And looked about her sullenly.
"I'm cold ... I'm mortal cold," she said:
"What call had you to waken me?
I was so warm and happy, dead...
And still those staring stars!" Her head
Dropt in her hands: and thick and fast
The tears came with a heavy sobbing.
He stood quite helpless while she cried;
And watched her shaken bosom throbbing
With passionate, wild, weak distress,
Till it was spent. And then she dried
Her eyes upon her singed black dress;
Looked up, and saw him standing there,
Wondering, and more than half-afraid.
But now, the nipping, hungry air
Took hold of her, and struck fear dead.
She only felt the starving sting
That must, at any price, be stayed;
And cried out: "I am famishing!"
Then from his pocket he took bread
That he had been too weak and sick
To eat o'ernight: and eager-eyed,
She took it timidly; and said:
"I have not tasted food two days."
And, as he waited by her side,
He watched her with a quiet gaze;
And saw her munch the broken crust
So gladly, seated in the dust
Of that black desert's bitter night,

Beneath the freezing stars, so white
And hunger-pinched: and at the sight
Keen pity touched him to the quick;
Although he never said a word,
Till she had finished every crumb.
And then he led her to a seat
A little closer to the heat,
But well beyond the deadly stife.
And in the ashes, side by side,
They sat together, dazed and dumb,
With eyes upon the ovens' glare,
Each looking nakedly on life.
And then, at length, she sighed, and stirred,
Still staring deep and dreamy-eyed
Into the whitening, steady glow.
With jerky, broken words and slow,
And biting at her finger-ends,
She talked at last: and spoke out all
Quite open-heartedly, as though
There were not any stranger there--
The fire and he, both bosom-friends.
She'd left her home three months ago--
She, country-born and country-bred,
Had got the notion in her head
That she'd like city-service best...
And so no country place could please...
And she had worried without rest
Until, at last, she got her ends;
And, wiser than her folk and friends,
She left her home among the trees...
The trees grew thick for miles about
Her father's house ... the forest spread
As far as ever you could see...
And it was green, in Summer, green...

Since she had left her home, she'd seen
No greenness could compare with it...
And everything was fresh and clean,
And not all smutched and smirched with smoke
They burned no sooty coal and coke,
But only wood-logs, ash and oak...
And by the fire at night they'd sit...
Ah! wouldn't it be rare and good
To smell the sappy, sizzling wood,
Once more; and listen to the stream
That runs just by the garden-gate...
And often, in a Winter spate,
She'd wakened from a troubled dream,
And lain in bed, and heard it roar;
And quaked to hear it, as a child...
It seemed so angry, and so wild--
Just mad to sweep the house away!
And now, it was three months or more
Since she had heard it, on the day...
The day she left ... and Michael stood...
He was a woodman, too, and he
Worked with her father in the wood...
And wanted her, she knew ... but she
Was proud, and thought herself too good
To marry any country lad...
'Twas queer to think she'd once been proud--
And such a little while ago--
A beggar, wolfing crusts! ... The pride
That made her quit her countryside
Soon left her stranded in the crowd...
And precious little pride she had
To keep her warm these freezing days
Since she had fled the city-ways
To walk back home ... aye! home again:

For, in the town, she'd tried in vain,
For honest work to earn her bread...
At one place, they'd nigh slaved her dead,
And starved her, too; and, when she left,
Had cheated her of half her wage:
But she'd no means to stop the theft...
And she'd had no more work to do...
Two months since, now ... it seemed an age!
How she had lived, she scarcely knew...
And still, poor fool, too proud to write
To home for help, until, at length,
She'd not a penny for a bite,
Or pride enough to clothe her back...
So, she was tramping home, too poor
To pay the train-fare ... she'd the strength,
If she'd the food ... but that hard track,
And that cold, cruel, bitter night
Had taken all the heart from her...
If Michael knew, she felt quite sure...
For she would rather drop stone-dead
Than live as some ... if she had cared
To feed upon the devil's bread,
She could have earned it easily...
She'd pride enough to starve instead,
Aye, starve, than fare as some girls fared...
But, that was all behind ... and she
Was going home ... and yet, maybe,
If they'd a home like hers, they, too,
Would be too proud ... she only knew
The thought of home had kept her straight,
And saved her ere it was too late.
She'd soon be home again...
And now
She sat with hand upon her brow;

And did not speak again nor stir.

And, as he heard her words, his gaze
Still set upon the steady glare,
His thoughts turned back to city-ways:
And he remembered common sights
That he had seen in city nights:
And, once again, in early June,
He wandered through the midnight street;
And heard those ever-pacing feet
Of young girls, children yet in years,
With gaudy ribbons in their hair,
And shameless fevered eyes astare,
And slack lips set in brazen leers,
Who walked the pavements of despair,
Beneath the fair full Summer moon...
Shadowed by worn-out, wizened hags,
With claw-hands clutching filthy rags
About old bosoms, shrunk and thin,
And mouths aleer without a tooth,
Who dogged them, cursing their sleek youth
That filched their custom and their bread...
Then, in a reek of hot gas light,
He stood where, through the Summer night,
Half-dozing in the stifling air,
The greasy landlord, fat with sin,
Sat, lolling in his easy chair,
Just half-way up the brothel stair,
To tax the earnings they brought in,
And hearken for the policeman's tread...

Then, shuddering back from that foul place
And turning from the ovens' glare,
He looked into her dreaming face;
And saw green, sunlit woodlands there,

And waters flashing in between
Low-drooping boughs of Summer green.

And as he looked, still in a dream
She murmured: "Michael would, she knew...
Though she'd been foolish ... he was true,
As true as steel, and fond of her...
And then she sat with eyes agleam
In dreaming silence, till the stir
Of cold dawn shivered through the air:
When, twisting up her tumbled hair,
She rose; and said, she must be gone.
Though she'd still far to go, the day
Would see her well upon her way...
And she had best be jogging on,
While she'd the strength ... and so, "Good-bye."

And as, beneath the paling sky,
He trudged again the cinder-track
That stretched before him, dead and black,
He muttered: "It's a chance the light
Has found me living still ... and she--
She, too ... and Michael ... and through me
God knows whom I may wake to-night."
1910-1911.